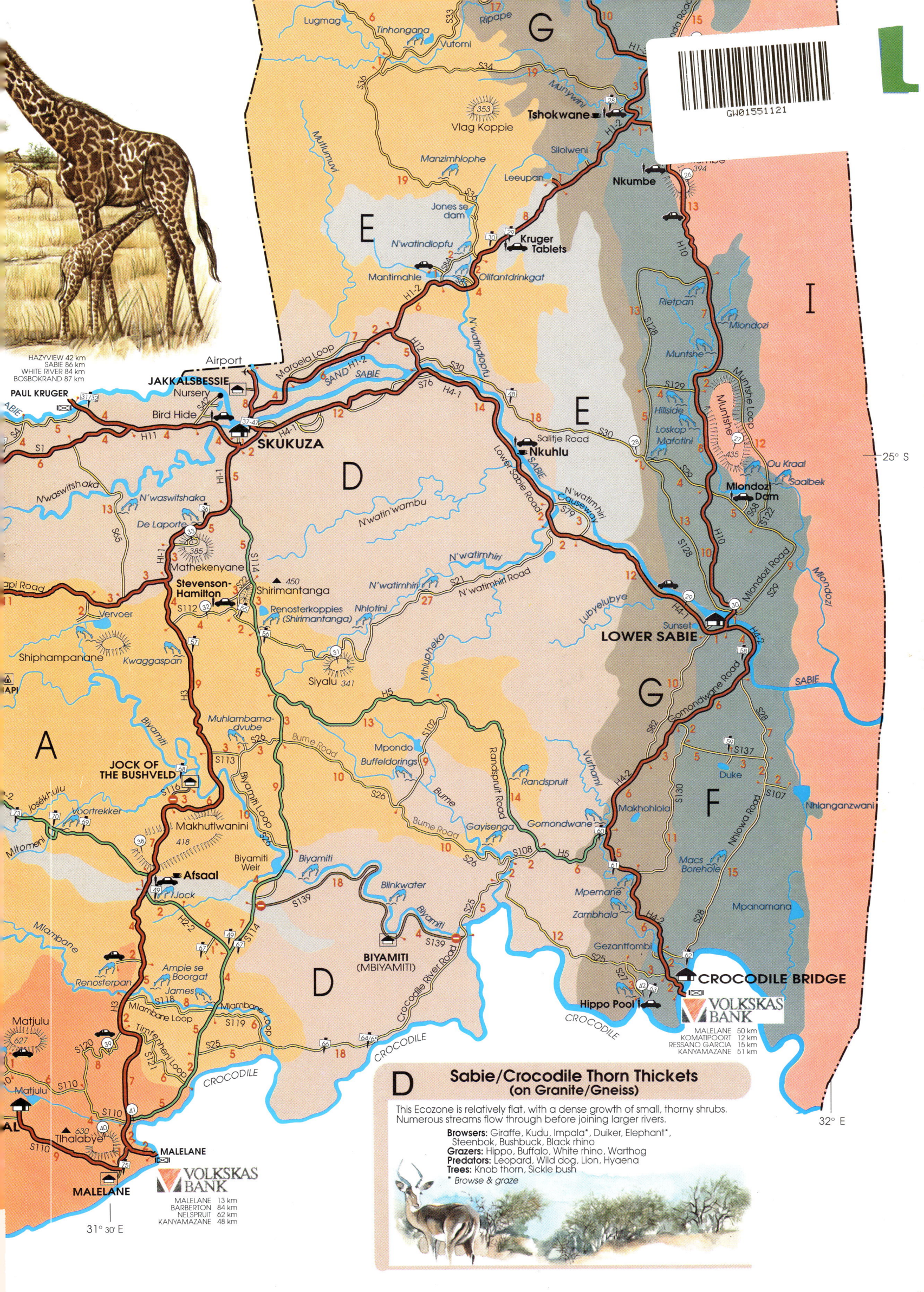

2 How to **Find It** using Ecozone Blocks

READ MAP 1 BEFORE READING THE INFORMATION BELOW

On these maps (and in the **Find It** Species Guide) there is a an Ecozone Block next to each animal. The colours and letters of these Blocks are the same as those on the **Map** and in the **Ecozone Information**.
The highlighted colours will show you the Ecozone on the **Map** where you are more likely to see the species. Grey in the Ecozone Blocks indicates where you are less likely to see the species.

A	E	I	M
B	F	J	N
C	G	K	O
D	H	L	P

TURN TO MAP 5 FOR MORE INFORMATION

Black rhino
Browsers, preferring thickets such as those between the Crocodile and Sabie Rivers.

A	E	I	M
B	F	J	N
C	G	K	O
D	H	L	P

A Mixed Bushwillow Woodlands (on Granite/Gneiss)

This Ecozone has gently sloping hills and valleys. Broad-leaved trees prefer the higher, upland areas while thorn trees prefer lower-lying areas. Many drainage lines of different sizes flow through this Ecozone.

Browsers: Giraffe, Kudu, Impala*, Duiker, Klipspringer, Steenbok
Grazers: Zebra, Buffalo, White rhino, Sable
Predators: Lion, Hyaena, Side-striped jackal
Trees: Bushwillow, Knob thorn
* Browse & graze

G Delagoa Thorn Thickets (on Ecca Shales)

There is often abundant game as the grass is very sweet. Patches of open grassveld, often bare through overgrazing, occur between dense thickets of Delagoa thorn trees.

Browsers: Giraffe, Kudu, Impala*, Duiker, Elephant*, Steenbok
Grazers: Zebra, Wildebeest, Buffalo, Waterbuck, White rhino
Predators: Cheetah, Lion, Hyaena, Leopard
Trees: Delagoa thorn, Many-stemmed false-thorn
* Browse & graze

E Thorn Veld (on Gabbro)

Scattered trees and wide open plains, covered by grassland which is very sweet and short, attracting herds of grazers.

Browsers: Giraffe, Kudu, Impala*, Duiker
Grazers: Buffalo, Zebra, Wildebeest, Warthog
Predators: Lion, Hyaena, Cheetah, Black-backed jackal
Trees: Marula, Large knob thorn
* Browse & graze

K Stunted Knob Thorn Savannah (on Basalt)

This area has flat basalt plains with very shallow soils. Large thickets of stunted knob thorn trees are common.

Browsers: Giraffe, Kudu, Impala*
Grazers: Zebra, Wildebeest, Buffalo, Sable
Predators: Cheetah, Lion, Hyaena
Trees: Stunted knob thorn, Leadwood
* Browse & graze

MAROELA
ORPEN

TZANEEN 180 km
WHITE RIVER 139 km
HOEDSPRUIT 66 km
BOSBOKRAND 84 km

VOLKSKAS BANK

F Knob Thorn/Marula Savannah (on Basalt)

Vast, flat, basalt plains have scattered large trees and shrubs. Soil is clay-based, resulting in pans of water forming after summer rains.

Browsers: Giraffe, Kudu
Grazers: Zebra, Wildebeest, Buffalo, Tsessebe, Waterbuck, Warthog
Predators: Cheetah, Lion, Hyaena, Black-backed jackal
Trees: Marula, Knob thorn

A	E	I	M
B	F	J	N
C	G	K	O
D	H	L	P

White rhino
Grazers, mostly found on gabbro and basalt in the south.

1 How to **Find It** using this **Map**

This **Map** is divided into Ecozones which will help you to find the major mammals and common trees more easily. The Ecozones are based on the underlying geology and rainfall.

Just follow these steps!
- Turn to the relevant **Map** section and find where you are.
- See which Ecozone you are in by the colour and the letter of the area. → D
- On the side of the **Map** find the **Ecozone Information** with the matching colour, letter and name. e.g.

  D **Sabie/Crocodile Thorn Thickets** (on Granite/Gneiss)

The **Ecozone Information** includes the underlying geology which determines the soil type.
- Most plants grow better in certain soils and are more common there.
- Animals prefer specific types of plants and will concentrate where their favourite food is to be found.
- Where two Ecozones meet, the vegetation of the two zones is likely to be mixed. Vegetation near koppies and rivers will also be mixed and less reliable.

Giraffe
More common in the south of the Park; can reach leaves too high for other browsers; prefer *Acacia* trees.

TURN TO MAPS 2 AND 5 FOR MORE INFORMATION

A Mixed Bushwillow Woodlands
(on Granite/Gneiss)

This Ecozone has gently sloping hills and valleys. Broad-leaved trees prefer the higher, upland areas while thorn trees prefer lower-lying areas. Many drainage lines of different sizes flow through this Ecozone.

Browsers: Giraffe, Kudu, Impala*, Duiker, Klipspringer, Steenbok
Grazers: Zebra, Buffalo, White rhino, Sable
Predators: Lion, Hyaena, Side-striped jackal
Trees: Bushwillow, Knob thorn
* Browse & graze

B Pretoriuskop Sourveld
(on Granite/Gneiss)

The gently sloping hills and valleys are covered with dense trees, shrubs and tall grass. This area also has scattered, impressive granite hills and koppies.

Browsers: Giraffe, Kudu, Impala*, Duiker, Klipspringer
Grazers: Common & Mountain reedbuck, White rhino, Sable
Predators: Wild dog, Lion, Side-striped jackal
Trees: Silver cluster-leaf, Rock fig
* Browse & graze

C Malelane Mountain Bushveld
(on Granite/Gneiss)

Many unusual plants grow in this mountainous landscape. The plains between the mountains are covered in sweet grass which attracts a variety of grazers.

Browsers: Duiker, Klipspringer, Kudu, Impala*
Grazers: Waterbuck, White rhino, Sable, Common & Mountain reedbuck
Trees: Red bushwillow, Magic guarri
* Browse & graze

- Riverine vegetation occurs around every river shown, although it has no letter reference or colour code on the **Map** itself.
- **Ecozone Information** for:

  E **F** G is on Map 2

  I is on Map 3

   is on Map 4

VOLKSKAS BANK

HAZYVIEW 19 km
WHITE RIVER 32 km
NELSPRUIT 51 km

NUMBI

Pretorius Kop 732
Manungu 689

Albasini Ruins

Phabeni
Mestel
Mtshawu

Albasini Road
Mtshawu

Matupa 504
Shabeni 759

Dolspane Road

Nyamundwa

Matlhari 451

Mlale

Napi 505

Shitlhave

PRETORIUSKOP

Biyamiti

E

Voortrekker Road
Ship Mountain 662
691
Sitfungwane

Komar

Newu 666
Mangaka
New

Stolsnek

Fayi Loop
Nsikazi

B

WOLHUTER

Matju
Matjulu

BOESMAN

Maqili 674

BERG-EN

Khandzali

Nsikazi

CROCODI

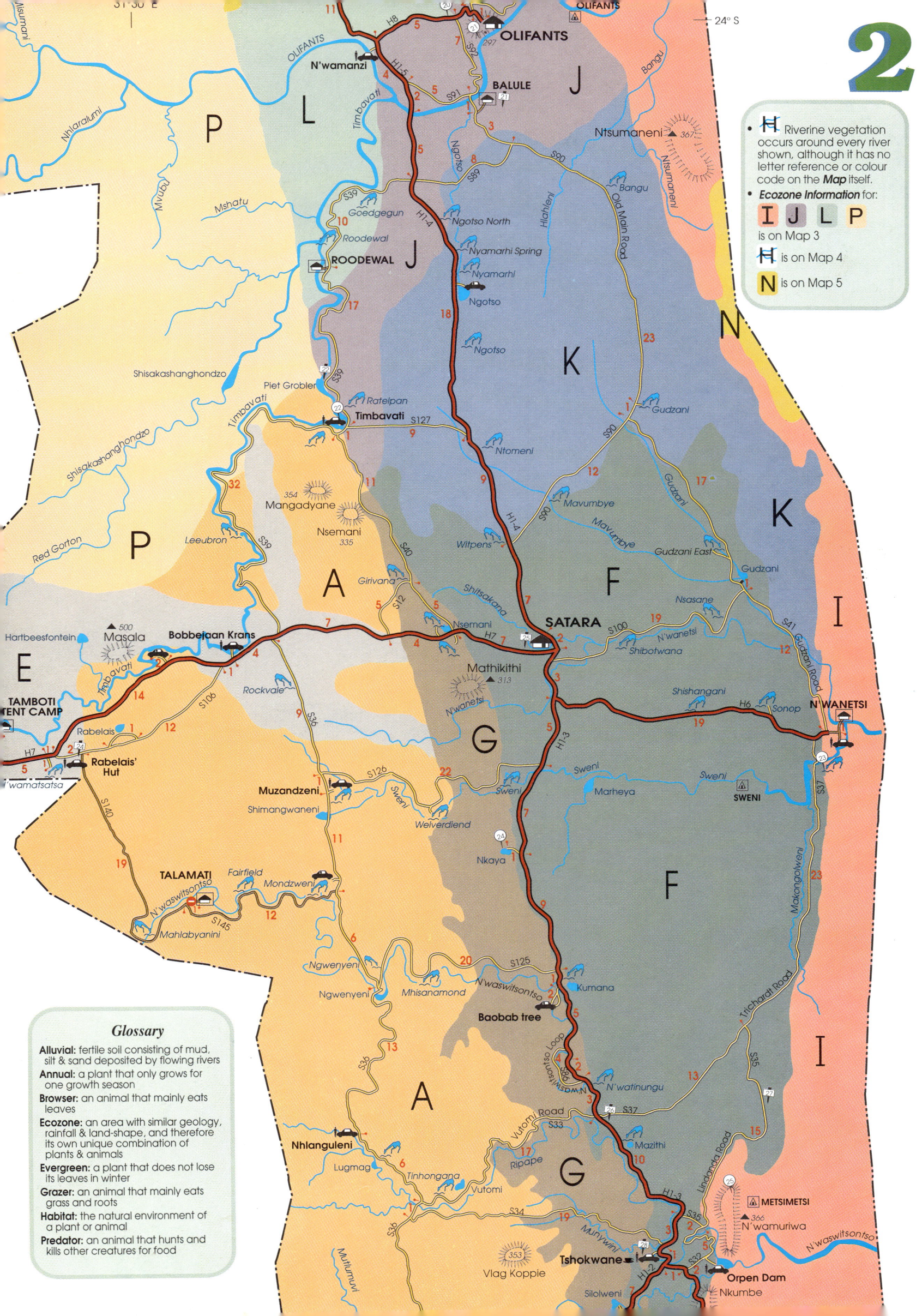

2

- Riverine vegetation occurs around every river shown, although it has no letter reference or colour code on the **Map** itself.
- *Ecozone Information* for:

  I **J** **L** **P** is on Map 3

  ⊔⊓ is on Map 4

  N is on Map 5

Glossary

Alluvial: fertile soil consisting of mud, silt & sand deposited by flowing rivers

Annual: a plant that only grows for one growth season

Browser: an animal that mainly eats leaves

Ecozone: an area with similar geology, rainfall & land-shape, and therefore its own unique combination of plants & animals

Evergreen: a plant that does not lose its leaves in winter

Grazer: an animal that mainly eats grass and roots

Habitat: the natural environment of a plant or animal

Predator: an animal that hunts and kills other creatures for food

3

How to **Find It** using this **Map**

PLEASE TURN TO MAPS 1, 2 AND 5 FOR INFORMATION →

I — Lebombo Mountain Bushveld (on Rhyolite)

The Lebombo Mountains are rugged with many rocky outcrops and deep ravines. They range over the whole length of Kruger, the north being drier than the south.

Browsers: Giraffe, Kudu, Impala*, Klipspringer
Grazers: Zebra, Buffalo, Waterbuck
Predators: Lion
Trees: Common tree Euphorbia, Baobab (north), Red bushwillow (south)
Browse & graze

J — Olifants Rugged Veld (on Rhyolite/Basalt)

Black boulders scattered across this Ecozone can give it a very harsh appearance in the dry months. After the rains annual plants appear.
Browsers: Giraffe, Kudu, Impala*, Elephant*, Klipspringer
Grazers: Zebra, Wildebeest
Predators: Lion, Hyaena
Trees: Thorny cluster-leaf, Raisin bush
Browse & graze

L — Mopane Shrubveld (on Basalt)

Typical of basalt soils, this Ecozone is flat with very few drainage lines. It has areas of dense mopane shrub and sparse grass cover.

Browsers: Elephant*, Steenbok, Eland, Sharpe's grysbok
Grazers: Zebra, Buffalo, Tsessebe, Roan, Sable
Predators: Lion, Leopard, Side-striped jackal
Trees: Shrub mopane, Apple-leaf
Browse & graze

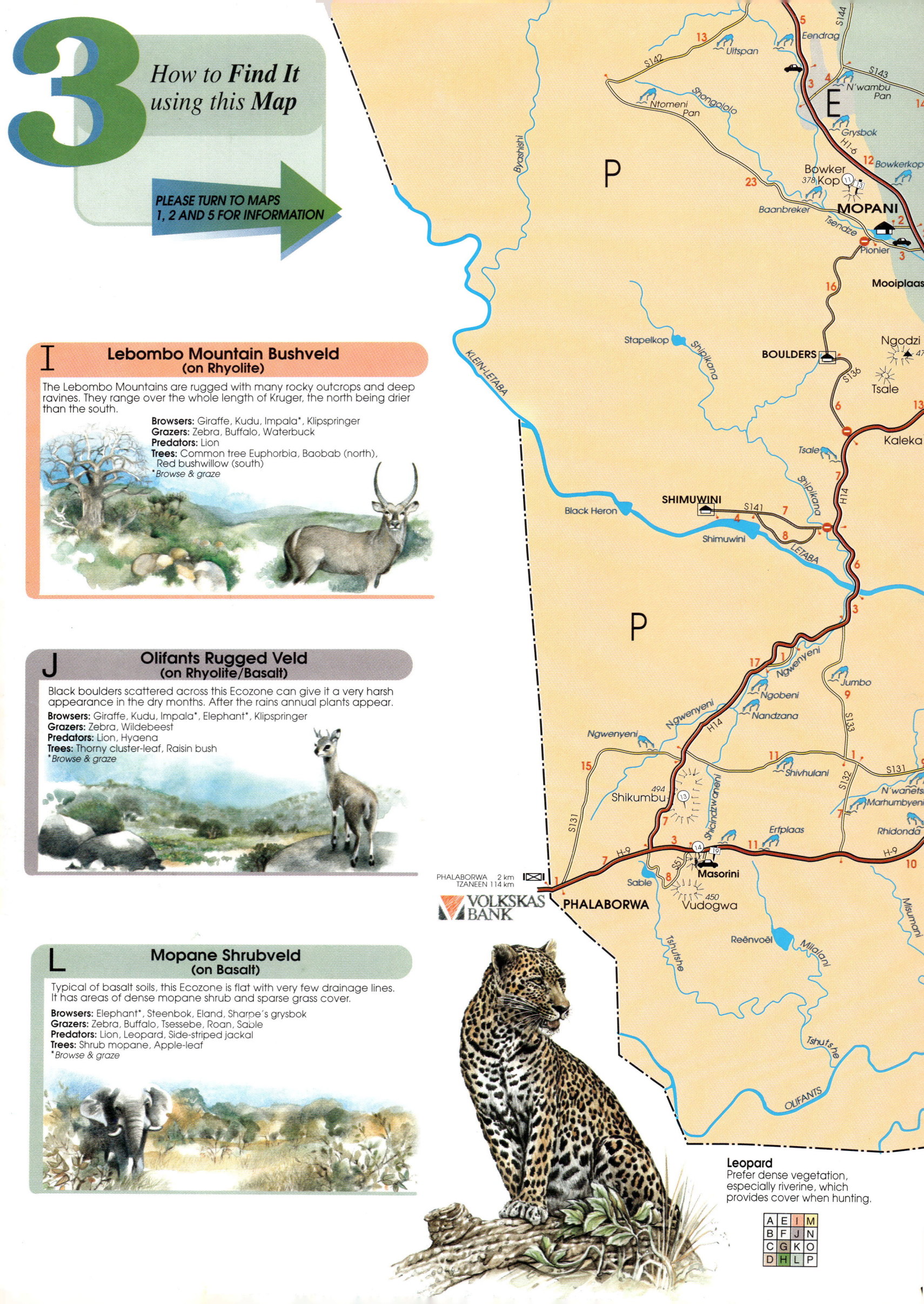

Leopard
Prefer dense vegetation, especially riverine, which provides cover when hunting.

PHALABORWA 2 km
TZANEEN 114 km

VOLKSKAS BANK

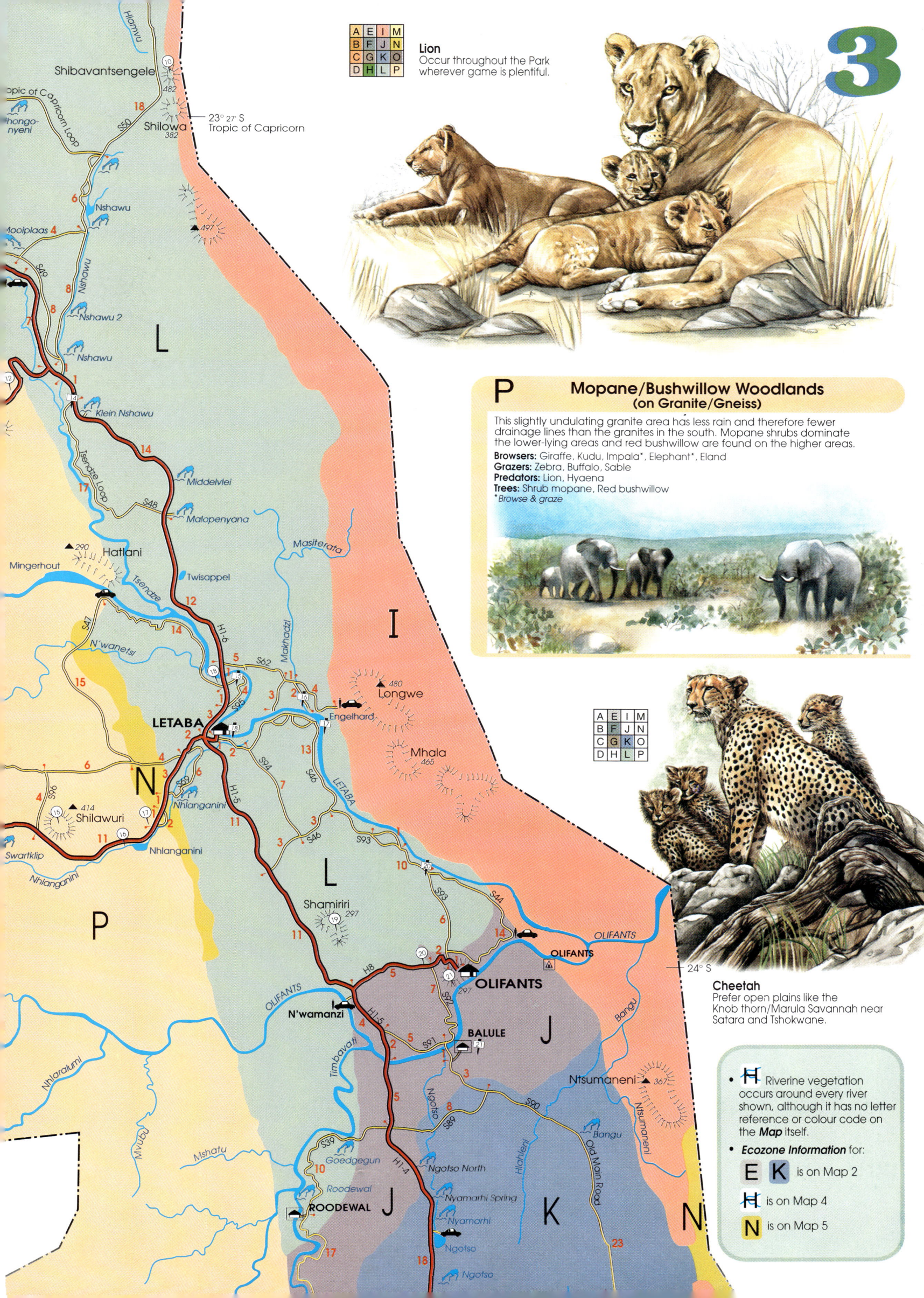

3

Lion
Occur throughout the Park wherever game is plentiful.

A	E	I	M
B	F	J	N
C	G	K	O
D	H	L	P

P — Mopane/Bushwillow Woodlands
(on Granite/Gneiss)

This slightly undulating granite area has less rain and therefore fewer drainage lines than the granites in the south. Mopane shrubs dominate the lower-lying areas and red bushwillow are found on the higher areas.

Browsers: Giraffe, Kudu, Impala*, Elephant*, Eland
Grazers: Zebra, Buffalo, Sable
Predators: Lion, Hyaena
Trees: Shrub mopane, Red bushwillow
*Browse & graze

A	E	I	M
B	F	J	N
C	G	K	O
D	H	L	P

Cheetah
Prefer open plains like the Knob thorn/Marula Savannah near Satara and Tshokwane.

- ⊢ Riverine vegetation occurs around every river shown, although it has no letter reference or colour code on the **Map** itself.
- **Ecozone Information** for:
  - E K is on Map 2
  - ⊢ is on Map 4
  - N is on Map 5

Shibavantsengele
Shilowa 382
23° 27' S Tropic of Capricorn
Tropic of Capricorn Loop
Phongo-nyeni
Mooiplaas
Nshawu
Nshawu 2
Nshawu
Klein Nshawu
Middelvlei
Matopenyana
Masiterata
Hatlani 290
Mingerhout
Twisappel
Tsendze Loop
N'wanetsi
Makhadzi
Longwe 480
Engelhard
Mhala 465
LETABA
Nhlanganini
Shilawuri 414
Swartklip
Nhlanganini
Nhlanganini
Shamiriri 297
OLIFANTS
N'wamanzi
Timbavati
OLIFANTS
OLIFANTS
BALULE
Ntsumaneni 367
Bangu
Bangu
Nhlaralumi
Mshatu
Goedgegun
Roodewal
ROODEWAL
Ngotso
Ngotso North
Nyamarhi Spring
Nyamarhi
Hlahleni
Old Main Road
Ngotso
Ngotso
24° S

L I N L P J K N

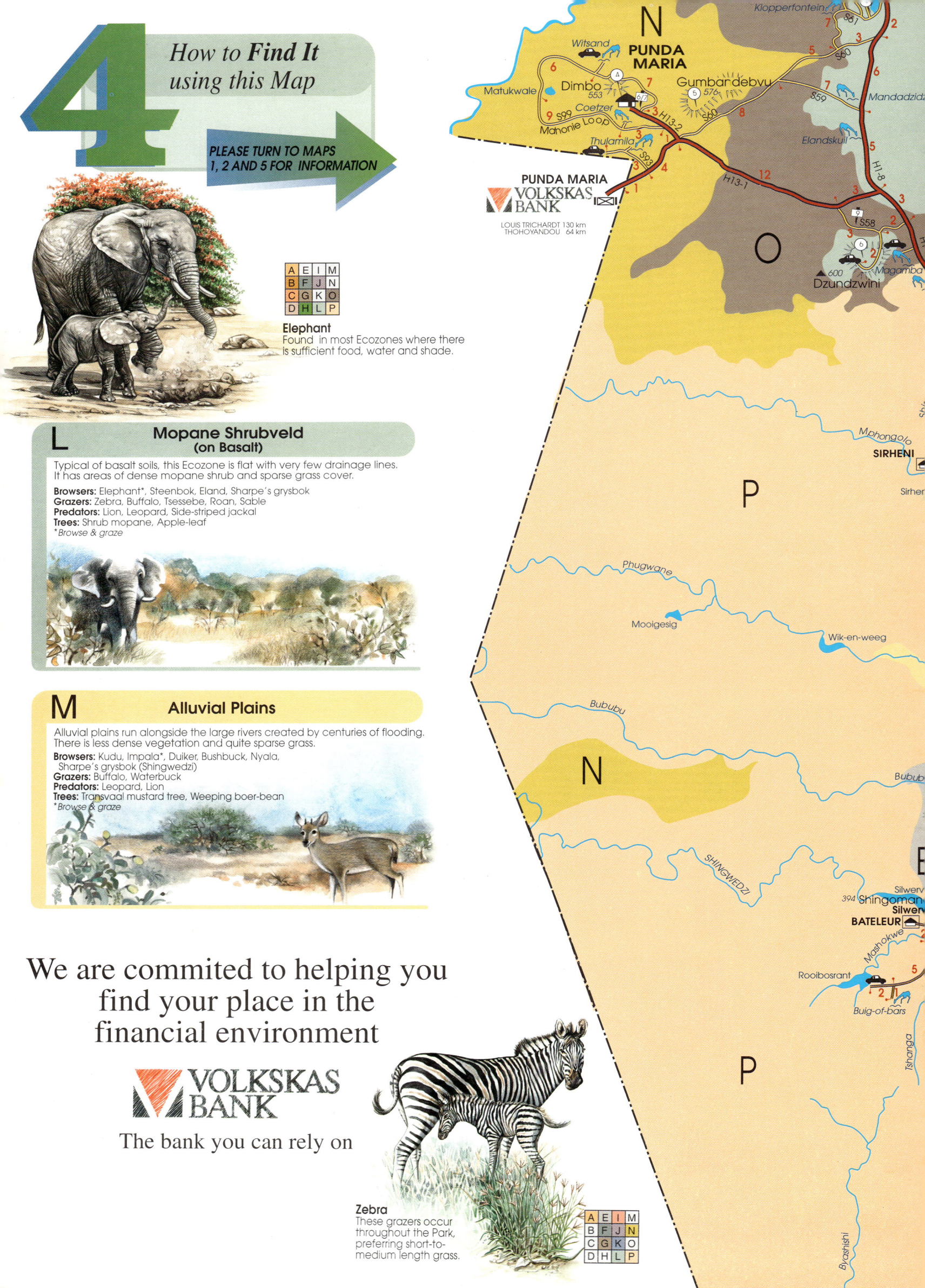

A	E	I	M
B	F	J	N
C	G	K	O
D	H	L	P

Elephant
Found in most Ecozones where there is sufficient food, water and shade.

L Mopane Shrubveld
(on Basalt)

Typical of basalt soils, this Ecozone is flat with very few drainage lines. It has areas of dense mopane shrub and sparse grass cover.

Browsers: Elephant*, Steenbok, Eland, Sharpe's grysbok
Grazers: Zebra, Buffalo, Tsessebe, Roan, Sable
Predators: Lion, Leopard, Side-striped jackal
Trees: Shrub mopane, Apple-leaf
*Browse & graze

M Alluvial Plains

Alluvial plains run alongside the large rivers created by centuries of flooding. There is less dense vegetation and quite sparse grass.

Browsers: Kudu, Impala*, Duiker, Bushbuck, Nyala, Sharpe's grysbok (Shingwedzi)
Grazers: Buffalo, Waterbuck
Predators: Leopard, Lion
Trees: Transvaal mustard tree, Weeping boer-bean
*Browse & graze

Zebra
These grazers occur throughout the Park, preferring short-to-medium length grass.

A	E	I	M
B	F	J	N
C	G	K	O
D	H	L	P

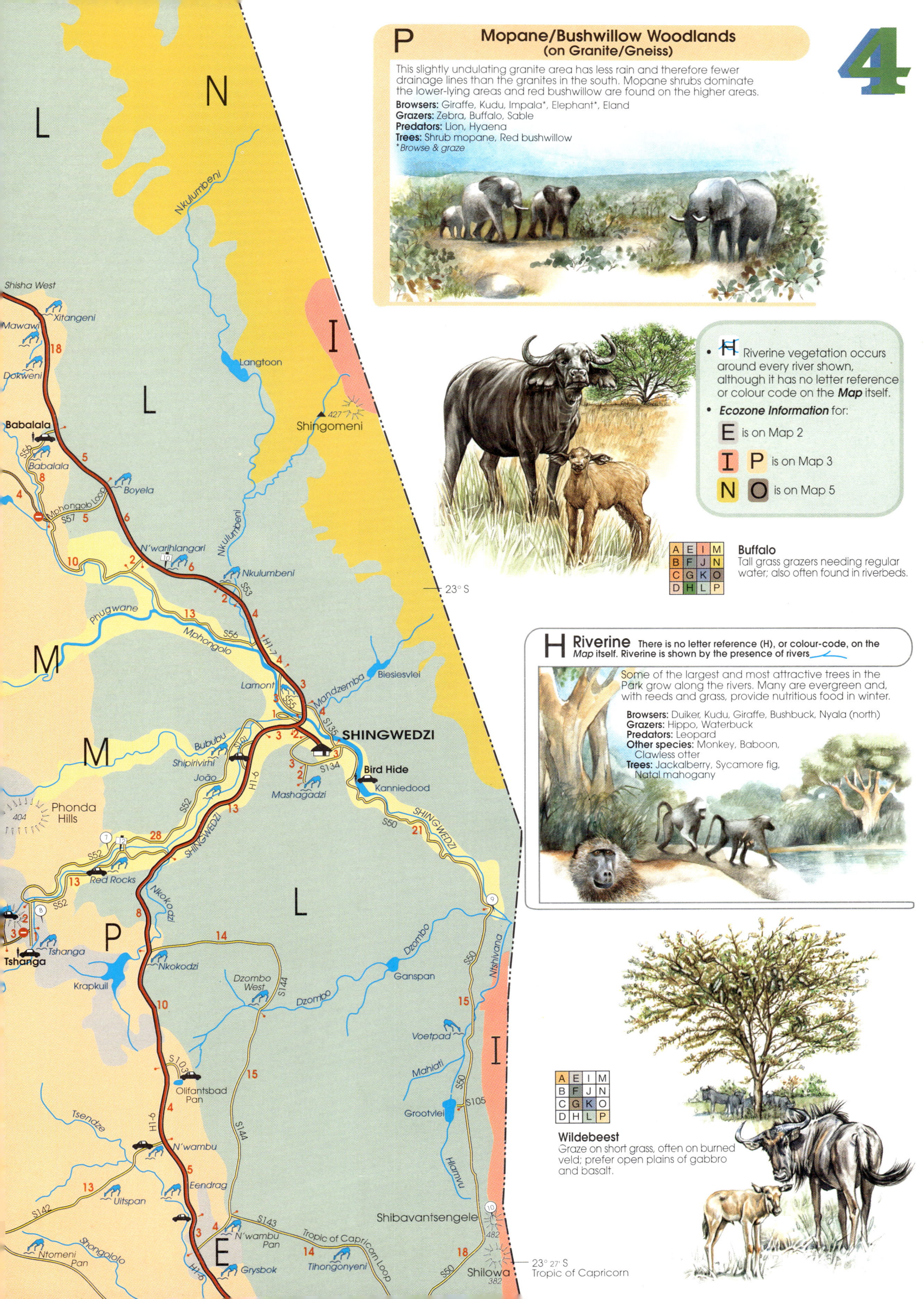

4

P — Mopane/Bushwillow Woodlands
(on Granite/Gneiss)

This slightly undulating granite area has less rain and therefore fewer drainage lines than the granites in the south. Mopane shrubs dominate the lower-lying areas and red bushwillow are found on the higher areas.

Browsers: Giraffe, Kudu, Impala*, Elephant*, Eland
Grazers: Zebra, Buffalo, Sable
Predators: Lion, Hyaena
Trees: Shrub mopane, Red bushwillow
Browse & graze

- **H** Riverine vegetation occurs around every river shown, although it has no letter reference or colour code on the **Map** itself.
- *Ecozone Information* for:

  E is on Map 2

  I **P** is on Map 3

  N **O** is on Map 5

A	E	I	M
B	F	J	N
C	G	K	O
D	H	L	P

Buffalo
Tall grass grazers needing regular water; also often found in riverbeds.

H — Riverine
There is no letter reference (H), or colour-code, on the **Map** itself. Riverine is shown by the presence of rivers

Some of the largest and most attractive trees in the Park grow along the rivers. Many are evergreen and, with reeds and grass, provide nutritious food in winter.

Browsers: Duiker, Kudu, Giraffe, Bushbuck, Nyala (north)
Grazers: Hippo, Waterbuck
Predators: Leopard
Other species: Monkey, Baboon, Clawless otter
Trees: Jackalberry, Sycamore fig, Natal mahogany

A	E	I	M
B	F	J	N
C	G	K	O
D	H	L	P

Wildebeest
Graze on short grass, often on burned veld; prefer open plains of gabbro and basalt.

Map labels

L N

Nkulumbeni

Shisha West
Mawawi · Xitangeni
Langtoon
Dokweni
18
L I
Babalala
Shingomeni ▲ 427
S56
Babalala
5
8
N'warihlangari
4
Boyela
Mphongolo Loop
S57
6
10
N'warihlangari 10
6
Nkulumbeni
2
S53
13
Phugwane
4
Mphongolo
S56
4 H1-7 4
M
Lamont
3
Mandzemba
Biesiesvlei
Bububu
S55
3
SHINGWEDZI
M
Shipirivirhi
2
S135
João
3
2
S134
Bird Hide
Mashagadzi
2
Kanniedood
Phonda Hills
404
S52
13
SHINGWEDZI
13
SHINGWEDZI
S50
21
28
Red Rocks
8
2
8
Nkokodzi
L
13
S52
2
Tshanga
3
14
Nkokodzi
P
Dzombo
Krapkuil
Dzombo West
S144
Ganspan
Ntshivana
9
10
Dzombo
15
S50
15
Voetpad
Olifantsbad Pan
S103
15
S144
Mahlati
S50
Tsendze
H1-6
Grootvlei
S105
N'wambu
5
13
Eendrag
Hlamvu
S142
Uitspan
S143
Shibavantsengele
10
Ntomeni Pan
Shongololo
N'wambu Pan
14
Tihongonyeni
482
E
H1-6
Grysbok
Shilowa
382
Tropic of Capricorn Loop
S50
18

23° S

23° 27' S
Tropic of Capricorn

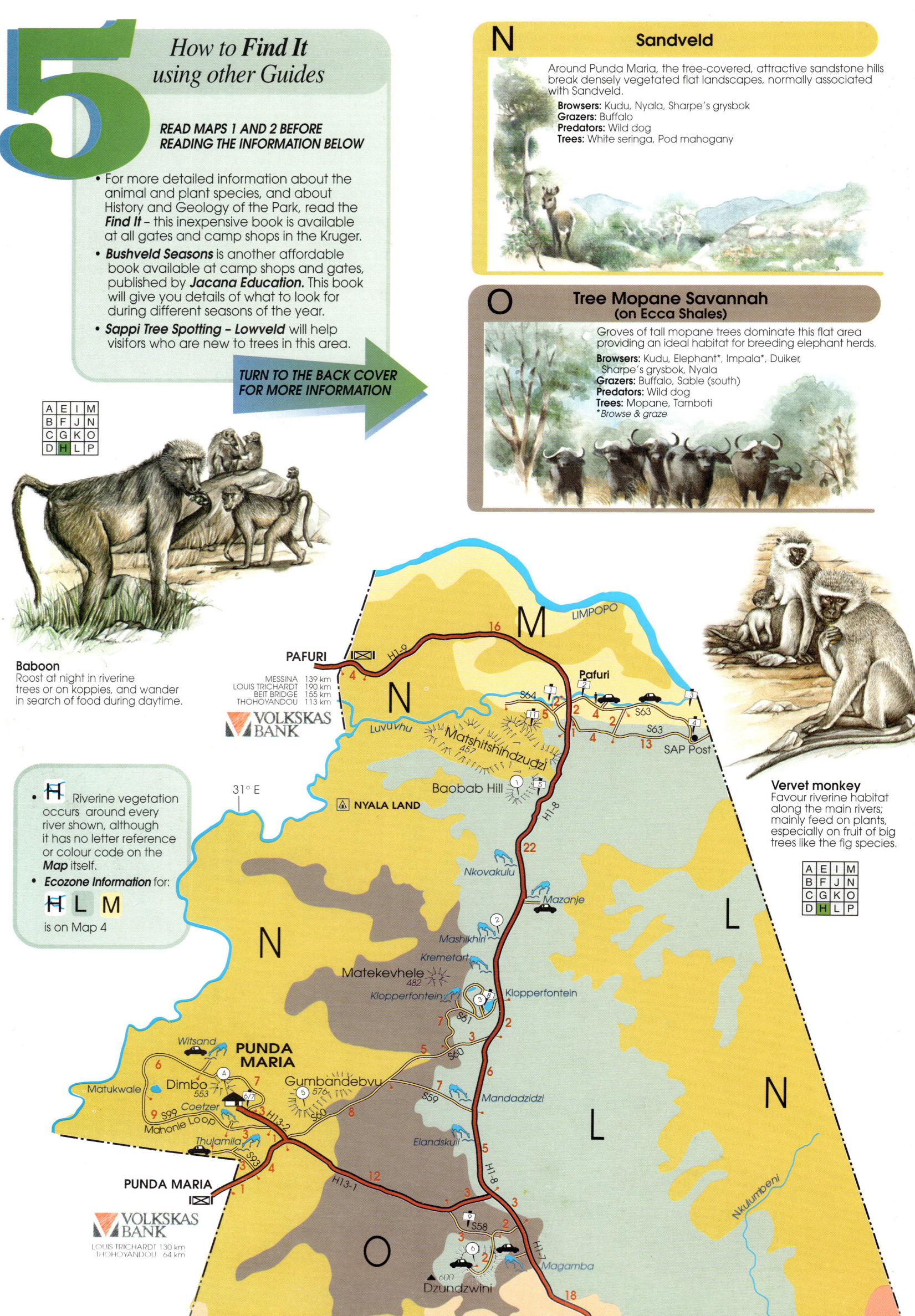

5 How to **Find It** using other Guides

READ MAPS 1 AND 2 BEFORE READING THE INFORMATION BELOW

- For more detailed information about the animal and plant species, and about History and Geology of the Park, read the **Find It** – this inexpensive book is available at all gates and camp shops in the Kruger.
- **Bushveld Seasons** is another affordable book available at camp shops and gates, published by **Jacana Education**. This book will give you details of what to look for during different seasons of the year.
- **Sappi Tree Spotting – Lowveld** will help visitors who are new to trees in this area.

TURN TO THE BACK COVER FOR MORE INFORMATION

N Sandveld

Around Punda Maria, the tree-covered, attractive sandstone hills break densely vegetated flat landscapes, normally associated with Sandveld.

Browsers: Kudu, Nyala, Sharpe's grysbok
Grazers: Buffalo
Predators: Wild dog
Trees: White seringa, Pod mahogany

O Tree Mopane Savannah (on Ecca Shales)

Groves of tall mopane trees dominate this flat area providing an ideal habitat for breeding elephant herds.

Browsers: Kudu, Elephant*, Impala*, Duiker, Sharpe's grysbok, Nyala
Grazers: Buffalo, Sable (south)
Predators: Wild dog
Trees: Mopane, Tamboti
*Browse & graze

Baboon
Roost at night in riverine trees or on koppies, and wander in search of food during daytime.

Vervet monkey
Favour riverine habitat along the main rivers; mainly feed on plants, especially on fruit of big trees like the fig species.

- H Riverine vegetation occurs around every river shown, although it has no letter reference or colour code on the **Map** itself.
- **Ecozone Information** for: H L M is on Map 4

PAFURI

MESSINA 139 km
LOUIS TRICHARDT 190 km
BEIT BRIDGE 155 km
THOHOYANDOU 113 km

VOLKSKAS BANK

31° E

NYALA LAND

Luvuvhu
Matshitshihdzudzi 457
Baobab Hill

LIMPOPO
16   M
Pafuri
SAP Post
S64
S63
13
22
Nkovakulu
Mazanje
Mashikhiri
Kremetart
Matekevhele 482
Klopperfontein
Klopperfontein
S61
Witsand
PUNDA MARIA
Dimbo 553
Matukwale
Coetzer
S99
Mahonie Loop
Thujamila
S23
Gumbandebvu 576
S60
Mandadzidzi
S59
Elandskuil
PUNDA MARIA
VOLKSKAS BANK
LOUIS TRICHARDT 130 km
THOHOYANDOU 64 km
H13-1
12
S58
Nkulumbeni
O
Magamba
Dzundzwini 600
18

N   N   N   L   N

REST CAMPS

	* Day visitor facilities	Camping and caravan	Conference facilities	Swimming pool (residents only)	In camp trail	Environmental educ. centre	Educational display	Petrol station	Car wash	AA Emergency services	Car hire	Airport	Shop	Restaurant/cafeteria	Bank	Post office	Telephone	Doctor	Laundromat
MAIN 🏠																			
Berg-en-dal	•	•	•	•	•	•	•						•	•			•		
Crocodile Bridge	•	•					•						•				•		•
Letaba	•	•			•		•	•		•			•	•		•	•		•
Lower Sabie		•					•						•	•		•	•		
Mopani	•		•	•	•		•						•	•		•	•		
Olifants	•				•								•	•			•		
Orpen	•												•	•		•	•		
Pretoriuskop	•	•		•	•	•							•	•		•	•		•
Punda Maria	•	•		•	•								•	•		•	•		
Satara	•	•				•		•	•	•			•	•		•	•		•
Shingwedzi	•	•		•		•							•	•		•	•		
Skukuza	•	•			•	•	•	•	•	•	•	•	•	•	•	•	•	•	•
OTHER 🏚																			
Private																			
Boulders																			
Jock of the Bushveld						•													
Malelane																			
N'wanetsi																			
Roodewal																			
Bushveld																			
Bateleur			•														•		
Biyamiti																	•		
Jakkalsbessie			•														•		
Shimuwini																	•		
Sirheni																	•		
Talamati																	•		
Camping																			
Balule		•																	
Maroela		•																	
Tamboti (Tent Camp)																			

*** Day visitor facilities** include toilets, shade, seating and braai area

---

GET-OUT POINTS & GATES

	Toilets	Shade	Seating	Braai area	Boiling water	Cooking gas	Cool drinks only	Shoplets/kiosk	Hot refreshments	Wood for sale	Telephone	Educational display
GET-OUT POINTS 🚗												
Afsaal 🍴	•	•	•	•	•		•	•	•	•		
Albasini Ruins											•	•
Babalala	•	•	•	•	•	•				•		
Bird Hide (Shingwedzi)		•	•								•	
Bird Hide (Skukuza)		•	•									
Bobbejaan Krans												
Hippo Pool												
Kruger Tablets												
Masorini	•	•	•	•	•							•
Mlondozi Dam	•	•	•							•		
Mooi Plaas	•	•	•	•						•		
Muzandzeni	•	•	•	•						•		
Nhlanguleni	•	•	•	•						•		
Nkuhlu 🍴	•	•	•	•			•	•				
Nkumbe	•	•	•									
N'wamanzi												
N'wanetsi	•	•	•	•						•		
Orpen Dam	•	•	•									
Pafuri Picnic	•	•	•	•								
Rabelais' Hut											•	
Stevenson-Hamilton												
Timbavati	•	•	•	•	•					•		
Tshanga	•	•										
Tshokwane 🍴	•	•	•	•	•		•	•				
GATES 🚪												
Crocodile Bridge	•	•	•	•			•	•		•	•	
Malelane	•	•	•	•		•				•		
Numbi	•	•	•	•	•	•				•		
Orpen	•	•	•	•						•		
Pafuri	•											
Paul Kruger	•											
Phalaborwa	•	•	•	•						•		
Punda Maria	•									•		

🍴 Main picnic place

VISITOR FACILITIES

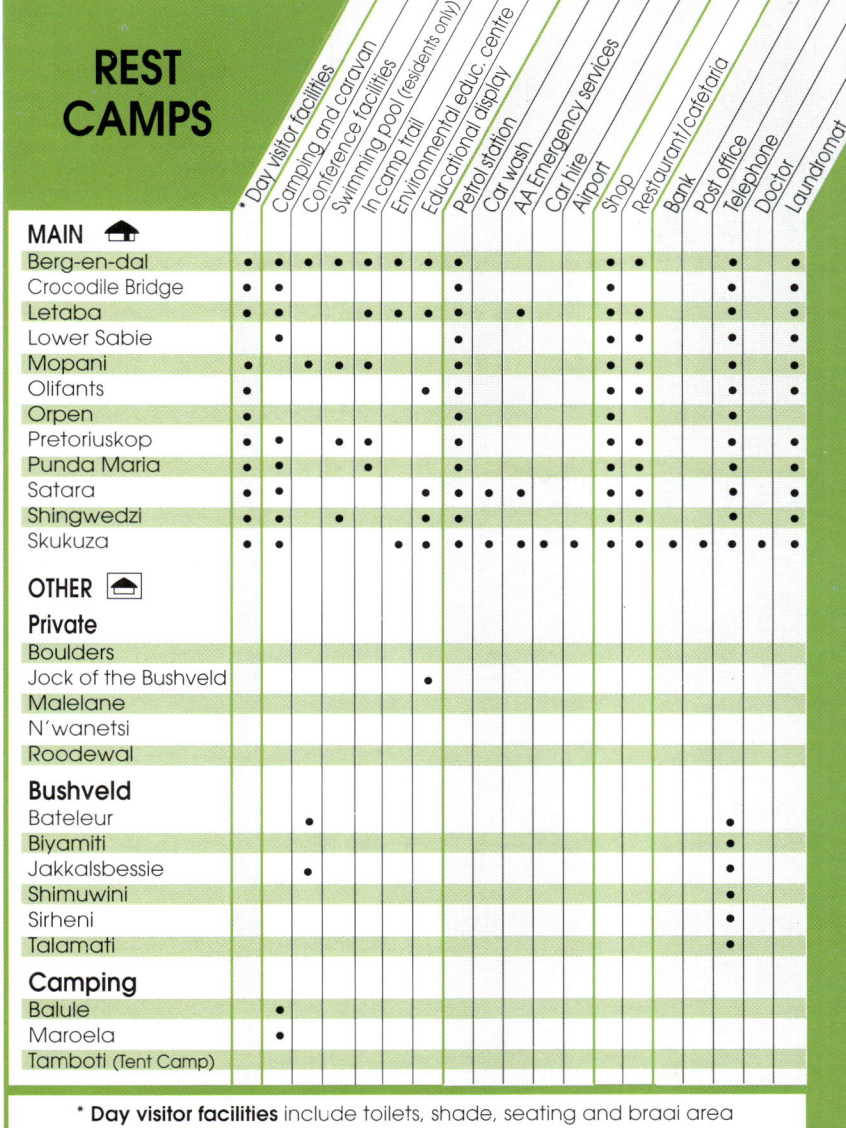

Hyaena
Common throughout the Park, but favour the central and southern Ecozones on basalt; usually scavenge at carcasses, but also efficient hunters.

A	E	I	M
B	F	J	N
C	G	K	O
D	H	L	P

Black-backed jackal
Not common anywhere, but prefer the drier areas and more open savannah; do not need to be close to permanent water.

A	E	I	M
B	F	J	N
C	G	K	O
D	H	L	P

Wild dog
Due to hunting habits prefer open areas; tend to avoid areas favoured by lion, like basalt plains.

A	E	I	M
B	F	J	N
C	G	K	O
D	H	L	P

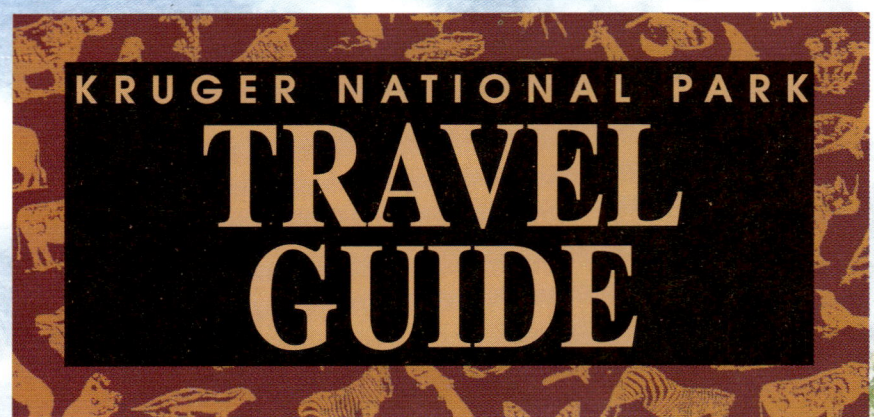

KRUGER NATIONAL PARK
TRAVEL GUIDE

Welcome to the
KRUGER NATIONAL PARK

WWF

Rock fig

Acacias

Planning your drive

Plan your drives carefully. There are no petrol stations and few rest rooms, toilets or shops between camps. Before you set off...
Be sure you have the following inside the car:
- an up-to-date map
- enough to eat and drink
- cameras, film, binoculars, reference books
- litter bag
  In addition be sure you have:
  - used the toilet
  - no necessities in the car boot
  - enough petrol, oil, water and correct tyre pressure (check your spare tyre)
  - checked the notice board outside camp reception for specific information of the day eg. some roads may be temporarily closed

Leopard
Eats anything from insects to buck three times its own weight. Solitary animal, the males associating with females only when breeding. Lives in diverse habitats, even near human settlements.

Kruger National Park is one of the last wild areas in South Africa. It offers the majesty of the African bush, the excitement of the 'Big Five', dramatic seasonal changes and a chance for both adventure and relaxation. This brochure gives useful information and fascinating facts, tips and advice that will make your Kruger experience more rewarding.
Enjoy your visit!

Klipspringer
Flat tips of hooves adapted to rocky areas. Water-independent. Main predators are leopard, but lambs are taken by eagles and baboons.

The buck stops here

The Park is not only a refuge for wildlife but it is also your National Park. It is **your** responsibility to look after it. Please obey all the Park rules. They are here for your benefit and safety too.

Giant plated lizard
This shy lizard measures up to 80 cm in length. Often seen after rain eating termites.

Do not pick things, damage them or take them away. Try not to change anything.

LIONS!
L-I-O-N-S stands for
Learn – Interpret – Observe – Never – Slow.
The tips below will help you to see more, and might even lead you to the king of the animals.
- **Learn** as much as you can before your drive. Read books like *Make the Most of Kruger, Bushveld Seasons* and the *Find It.* These books are available at low cost at the Park's shops and will increase your knowledge and chances of discovery. There are many books, tapes or videos that will add to your experience.
- **Interpre**t what you read and what you see by using your senses.
- **Observe** carefully by stopping often and waiting patiently.
- **Never** disobey the Park rules. They are there for your safety and benefit, as well as that of the Park's.
- **Slow** down. This is the best way to see more.

Redcrested korhaan
Male korhaan flies up vertically 20 m in display, then plunges straight down as if shot.

Animal Tracks: Hind = (h), Front = (f)

Leopard
9.5 cm

Giant plated lizard

Klipspringer
2 cm

Redcrested korhaan
3.9 cm

The Park's main aims

Kruger is one of the largest wildlife sanctuaries in the world. Its main aim is to conserve a unique part of nature as a natural, functioning system. The Park also plays an important role in education, recreation and tourism.

Census

Part of Kruger's research and management involves counting the major herbivores (plant-eaters) on a regular basis.
These populations change from year to year, depending mainly on rainfall and disease. This information influences management decisions and helps us understand population trends in the Park.
The last complete KNP census was done in 1993.

Brown snake eagle
Distinctive markings in flight with dual coloured wing-patterns. When sitting has large, square-shaped head.

	1981	1987	1990	1993
Blue wildebeest	9690	14600	14290	12720
Buffalo	34910	29710	27860	14230
Eland	560	990	740	490
Elephant	7340	6900	7280	7830
Giraffe	4960	4960	4720	4900
Hippo	unavailable	2770	2620	2140
Impala	121410	120350	116220	97290
Kudu	10290	8790	5970	3150
Roan antelope	340	280	170	40
Sable antelope	1860	2200	1880	880
Tsessebe	860	890	710	360
Warthog	4350	2980	2720	720
Waterbuck	3880	4020	3200	1430
White rhino	600	1020	1380	1870
Zebra	23980	32200	31910	29140

For animal census graphs, see the following page.

Lion	±2 000
Hyaena	±2 000
Leopard	±1 000
Wild dog	±380
Cheetah	±200

Never feed any kind of animal – this includes birds, monkeys, baboons, hyaenas – however tame they seem to be.

Impala
Scent glands behind the ankles confuse predators trying to single out an individual. Can jump 11 m across and 3 m high when fleeing.

Acacia

Hyaena
Females are dominant and bigger than males, but otherwise difficult to identify the sexes. Can digest bones, horns, hooves, even teeth within 24 hours.

Take a break

It is a good idea to stop often, if possible near a game path or a waterhole, even if there is nothing obvious to see. If you switch your engine and air conditioner off, and wait quietly, you will almost always be rewarded. It is safest to stop quite a distance away from elephants with young, particularly if your engine is turned off. Elephant cows can be very aggressive when separated from their young by a vehicle.

Slow approach

When you see another car ahead of you that has stopped, approach slowly and quietly, so you do not risk spoiling an excellent sighting.
When approaching a waterhole, it is essential to slow down and keep noise and movement to a minimum.

The tortoise and the hare

Remember the children's story of the tortoise who beat the speedy hare in a race? To see as many animals as possible, slow down, relax, and drive like a tortoise. The speed limit on tar roads is 50 km/h, but because animals are camouflaged, you will not see much at this speed. Speeding also scares game away and there is always a chance of hitting an animal. If you're serious about game-viewing, rather drive at under 20 km/h. Tortoise-time will win the day for you!

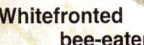

Whitefronted bee-eater
Nesting holes are 1 m long, in sandbanks. Colonies breed from Sept-Oct.

Acacia

Impala 5,5 cm

Hyaena
(h) 8 cm,
((f) 10 cm

Animal census totals KNP 1980-1993

Chart labels: Impala; Roan antelope; Blue wildebeest; Kudu / Elephant; Giraffe / Waterbuck; White rhino / Sable antelope; Tsessebe / Eland; Hippo / Warthog; Zebra / Buffalo

Kruger and research

Kruger's research programme is aimed at improving the management of the Park. New data also increases environmental awareness and education, even for people who live in towns and cities. It helps us appreciate the value of nature and teaches us that conservation is a vital part of the economy.

Kruger and the outside world

Scientific research looks at the inter-relationships of plant and animal species which helps Park management. It also benefits other conservation areas, farmers and communities living nearby, who have similar weather, soil and altitude to Kruger.

Leadwood

Leadwood

Elephant
Adults eat up to 200 kg of food a day. Related females suckle calves. Can communicate over vast distances using subsonic sound.

Wild dog
Has a vast home-range. Known to travel up to 80 km per day. Endangered due to pressure on territory and susceptibility to disease (rabies, distemper).

Wild date palm

Good timing

The best times for game-viewing are early morning and late afternoon, because many animals go down to the river to drink. If you are out during the hot midday period, follow the animals' example – find a shady spot near a riverbed or waterhole, and wait quietly.

Read the bush signs

Once you have stopped, look around carefully for tell-tale signs... the flick of an ear; fresh dung or spoor next to the road; a blur of movement deep in the bush; flattened grass tells where an animal may have rested. Also look for signs of recent feeding, which are especially obvious with elephants and recent kills.

Crested francolin
Feeds mostly on insects and bulbs found by scratching around in undergrowth. Cocks tail vertically like a bantam.

Malaria

Kruger is in a malaria area. Anti-malaria tablets should be taken before, during and after your visit.
Read the dosage instructions carefully. Mosquito repellent should be applied, especially in the summer at dawn and dusk. The malaria parasite takes about two weeks to incubate. Consult your doctor immediately if you experience symptoms of 'flu' after your visit to the Park.

Elephant (h) 52 cm (f) 50 cm

Wild dog 8 cm

Crested francolin

Camp life

Kruger's rest camps are the best places to see certain animals and plants at very close range. Bird-watching can be very rewarding in camp, as well as the fascinating world of insects, lizards, bats and squirrels, to mention a few.

Trees for life

Trees can be like old friends once you get to know them. It is always very rewarding to recognise them in the veld. Apart from their beauty, many have fascinating magical and medicinal properties. Many trees in camp have labels and the national tree numbers to help you identify them. Books are available at the shops to help you learn more. Look out for **Sappi tree spotting** in the Park shops.

Movies and information

Many camps have films at night which explore many aspects of the exciting and interesting creatures that live in the Park.
Visit the information centres at Berg-en-dal, Skukuza and Letaba.

Giant eagle owl
Largest southern African owl with a wingspan of up to 1,55 m. Prefers large trees next to rivers and streams.

Vervet monkey
Newcomers are not welcomed by a troop and are often viciously attacked.

Waterbuck
Greasy coat emits a musky, pungent smell. Rely on hiding from predators as they lack speed.

Read your Entry/Exit permit for more information on the Park rules.

Night life
Many creatures, from fascinating insects to large predators, come to life at night. Take a walk along the fence with your torch and look for nocturnal animals like genets, civets, nightjars, hyaenas or even lions. Listening to the incredible sounds of the African night is a unique experience. And so is looking up at the stars from the African soil!

Baboon
Complex social hierarchy. Females spend half their adult lives rearing young, and a third of their lives pregnant; have swollen red backsides when in season.

Python
Usually seen basking in the sun, but are more active at night. Hunt hares, rodents and even small antelope.

African bee
Normally only sting when agitated. During the dry season, concentrate at picnic spots in search of sweet substances and water. Keep cold drink tins covered.

Vervet monkey 5.5 cm

Python

Baboon (h) 15.5 cm, (f) 8.5 cm

Waterbuck 9 cm

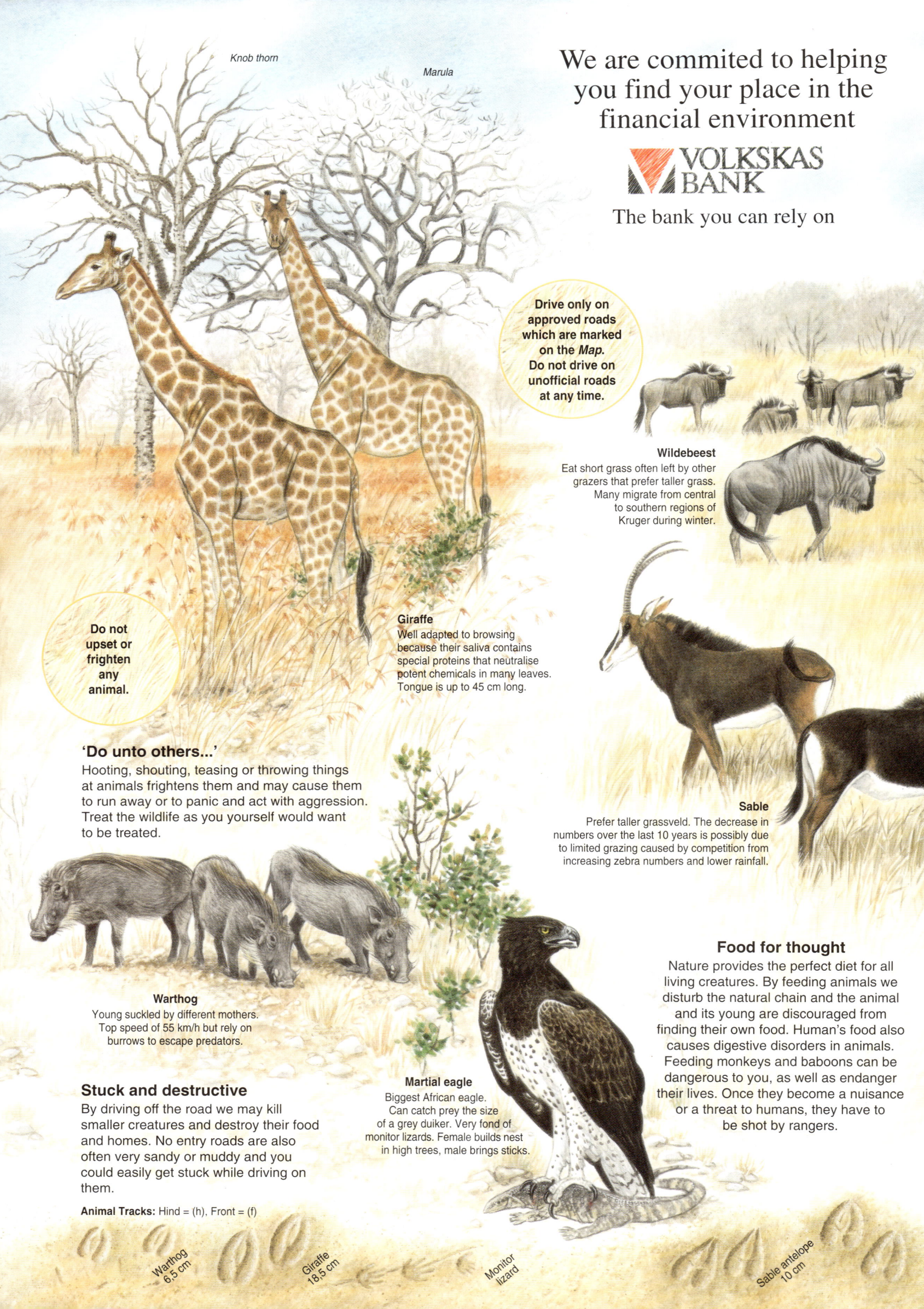

Knob thorn

Marula

Drive only on
approved roads
which are marked
on the *Map*.
Do not drive on
unofficial roads
at any time.

Wildebeest
Eat short grass often left by other
grazers that prefer taller grass.
Many migrate from central
to southern regions of
Kruger during winter.

Do not
upset or
frighten
any
animal.

Giraffe
Well adapted to browsing
because their saliva contains
special proteins that neutralise
potent chemicals in many leaves.
Tongue is up to 45 cm long.

Sable
Prefer taller grassveld. The decrease in
numbers over the last 10 years is possibly due
to limited grazing caused by competition from
increasing zebra numbers and lower rainfall.

'Do unto others...'
Hooting, shouting, teasing or throwing things
at animals frightens them and may cause them
to run away or to panic and act with aggression.
Treat the wildlife as you yourself would want
to be treated.

Food for thought
Nature provides the perfect diet for all
living creatures. By feeding animals we
disturb the natural chain and the animal
and its young are discouraged from
finding their own food. Human's food also
causes digestive disorders in animals.
Feeding monkeys and baboons can be
dangerous to you, as well as endanger
their lives. Once they become a nuisance
or a threat to humans, they have to
be shot by rangers.

Warthog
Young suckled by different mothers.
Top speed of 55 km/h but rely on
burrows to escape predators.

Stuck and destructive
By driving off the road we may kill
smaller creatures and destroy their food
and homes. No entry roads are also
often very sandy or muddy and you
could easily get stuck while driving on
them.

Animal Tracks: Hind = (h), Front = (f)

Martial eagle
Biggest African eagle.
Can catch prey the size
of a grey duiker. Very fond of
monitor lizards. Female builds nest
in high trees, male brings sticks.

Warthog
6,5 cm

Giraffe
18,5 cm

Monitor
lizard

Sable antelope
10 cm

Pace and peace

Sudden movements will often frighten animals away. Keep still and you will observe their natural behaviour. You will also start to feel the pace and peace of the bushveld and realise that here there is no predictable rush hour...only the occasional dash of speed when a predator is around.

Tree mopane

Shrub mopane

Ostrich
Male call is a deep booming sound. Can reach speeds up to 40 km/h.

Speed limit
Tarred Roads
50 km/h
Untarred Roads
40 km/h
Within Rest Camps
10 km/h

Buffalo
About 10 minutes after birth, calves can stand but can only keep up with herd after several weeks. Mothers and calves are often left behind and go into hiding.

Cheetah
Attain speeds up to 112 km/h but only for very short distances due to exhaustion and overheating. Cubs are often moved to avoid detection by hyaena, lion, leopard.

Ground hornbill
Like other hornbills these birds breed in holes in trees (Oct-Nov). Female is not plastered into the hole like other hornbill females, but is fed by her mate while nesting.

Gate times
Unless indicated, these times are for both *Entry* and *Camp* gates.

	Jan	Feb	Mar	Apr	May-Jul	Aug	Sept	Oct	Nov-Dec
Open	04:30 (camp gate) 05:30 (entry gate)	05:30	05:30	06:00	06:00	06:00	06:00	05:30	04:30 (camp gate) 05:30 (entry gate)
Close	18:30	18:30	18:00	18:00	17:30	18:00	18:00	18:00	18:30

Ostrich 17 cm

Cheetah 8.5 cm

Buffalo 13 cm

Ground hornbill 15.5 cm

Litter-bugs go home

Litter is life threatening. Plastic, broken bottles, tins and other rubbish can cause death. Even an apple core thrown onto the road can attract animals out of their natural habitat and they may be run over. Please help management by using the rubbish bag you received at the gate. All refuse in Kruger is sorted into degradable and non-degradable rubbish. This is essential in today's world, and perhaps, if you have not done so already, you can follow Kruger's recycling example at home.

Put all your litter into a rubbish bin, and be sure to close the lid properly.

Noise pollution

Not only litter, but loud radios and intrusive parties spoil the harmony of Kruger and ruin other people's enjoyment. When you leave you should be able to take some of the pace, the wisdom and the tranquility of the bush home with you.

African fish eagle
Both the male and female call, often early in the morning and especially in flight. These birds mate for life; only mature at 5 years.

Zebra
No individual zebra has the same pattern. Stripes are thought to confuse predators who cannot single out an individual. Dominant males 'keep' up to 7 females during mating season.

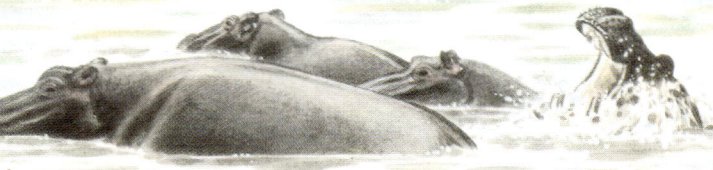

Hippopotamus
Mucous glands secrete oily red fluid to protect the thin, hairless skin from sunburn.

Extra vision

Use binoculars as often as possible, to scan an area for game, or to see something small or more specific. Animals move into deep shade during the hot midday hours, and are usually completely still. If you are out at this time, follow their example and find a shady spot, perhaps near a river or waterhole, and wait quietly.

Animal manners

Usually we say that someone with bad manners behaves like an animal. But in Kruger it is a good idea to watch animal's good behaviour and learn from it.

- Notice the order of their social structure and the interactions between individuals.
- Watch their excellent teamwork and communication.
- See how they teach their young the discipline and order which creates harmony and secures survival.
- Notice how efficiently they move and how aware they are of their surroundings.
- Be aware that nature wastes nothing.

Lion
Only about 20% of young survive due to starvation and predators (mainly hyaena). New males sometimes kill the young of defeated rivals, ensuring survival of strongest genes.

Zebra 10 cm

Hippo 25 cm

Lion 12 cm

Looking and seeing

Looking and seeing are two different things in the bush. You can look all day and see very little. Try to look deeper into the undergrowth for signs of movement or unusual shapes. It takes practice to see through dense bush, but each day you will increase your skills. Remember to look in trees for a leopard resting, or a large bird of prey. Scan the sky from time to time to see if vultures are circling, possibly above a kill.

Breaking the shape

Animals are used to the shape of vehicles. However if you break the outline of the vehicle's shape, by suddenly putting your arm or head out of the window, or by opening the doors, you may frighten them away or cause them to panic. Remember to stay in your vehicle at all times, unless in camps or official areas marked with the symbol ⬤ on the *Map*.

Sycamore fig

a palm

Lala palm

Kudu
Rely on camouflage in dense bush to escape predation. Bulls associate in bachelor herds when it is not breeding season.

Unless you are in a camp or at an area marked ⬤ on the *Map*, you must stay in your car at all times.

Bushbuck
The only solitary, non-territorial antelope in Kruger; only rams have horns and can be very dangerous when cornered or wounded.

Be sense-able

You will get more value from your drive if you use all your senses, not only your sight. Whenever possible drive without your air conditioner on, with your windows down. When you have stopped your car, listen, smell and look carefully. The smells and sounds of the bush give excellent clues which you would not notice from a moving vehicle...a nearby snort or bark; the nervous chattering of monkeys or birds; a different smell on the breeze! Listen carefully to the noises of nature, and in time you will learn to interpret mating calls or alarm calls that give away the presence of a predator. When baboons or monkeys are close by, for your own safety wind your windows up.

Kudu
8,5 cm

Bushbuck
4,5 cm

DISTANCES AND APPROXIMATE TIMES TAKEN BETWEEN GATES AND MAIN REST CAMPS

e.g. Berg-en-dal to Skukuza: distance = 72 km; approximate time = 2 hours 55 minutes (2h55)

TIME ESTIMATED TRAVELLING AT 25 KM/H
Distances taken on shortest tarred routes – on sand roads these can sometimes be shorter.

From	Skukuza	Shingwedzi	Satara	Punda Maria	Pretoriuskop	Phalaborwa Gate	Paul Kruger Gate	Pafuri Gate	Orpen	Olifants	N'wanetsi	Numbi Gate	Mopani	Malelane	Lower Sabie	Letaba	Crocodile Bridge	Berg-en-dal
Berg-en-dal	72	344	165	415	92	285	83	453	213	219	180	97	281	12	113	234	149	•
	2h55	13h45	6h35	16h35	3h40	11h25	3h20	18h10	8h30	8h45	7h10	3h50	11h15	0h30	4h30	9h25	6h00	•
Crocodile Bridge	77	306	127	377	125	246	88	415	175	181	142	130	243	141	34	196	•	149
	3h05	12h15	5h05	15h05	5h00	9h50	3h30	16h35	7h00	7h15	5h40	5h10	9h45	5h40	1h20	7h50	•	6h00
Letaba	162	109	69	176	211	51	173	218	117	32	94	216	47	226	162	•	196	234
	6h30	4h20	2h45	7h00	8h25	2h00	6h55	8h45	4h40	1h20	3h45	8h40	1h55	9h00	6h30	•	7h50	9h25
Lower Sabie	43	271	93	342	90	213	53	380	141	147	108	95	209	105	•	162	34	113
	1h45	10h50	3h45	13h40	3h35	8h30	2h10	15h10	5h40	5h55	4h20	3h50	8h20	4h10	•	6h30	1h20	4h30
Malelane	64	333	156	408	85	277	74	444	204	210	170	94	272	•	105	226	141	12
	2h35	13h20	6h15	16h20	3h25	11h05	3h00	17h45	8h10	8h25	6h50	3h50	10h55	•	4h10	9h00	5h40	0h30
Mopani	209	63	116	130	258	74	220	172	164	86	141	263	•	272	209	47	243	281
	8h20	2h30	4h40	5h10	10h20	3h00	8h50	6h55	6h35	3h25	5h40	10h30	•	10h55	8h20	1h55	9h45	11h15
Numbi Gate	54	325	147	396	9	267	65	434	195	201	162	•	263	94	95	216	130	97
	2h10	13h00	5h55	15h50	0h20	10h40	2h35	17h20	7h50	8h00	6h30	•	10h30	3h50	3h50	8h40	5h10	3h50
N'wanetsi	108	203	25	274	156	145	119	312	63	79	•	162	141	170	108	94	142	180
	4h20	8h10	1h00	11h00	6h15	5h50	4h45	12h30	2h30	3h10	•	6h30	5h40	6h50	4h20	3h45	5h40	7h10
Olifants	147	141	54	212	195	83	158	250	102	•	79	201	86	210	147	32	181	219
	5h55	5h40	2h10	8h30	7h50	3h20	6h20	10h00	4h05	•	3h10	8h05	3h25	8h25	5h55	1h20	7h15	8h45
Orpen	137	226	48	297	184	167	152	335	•	102	63	195	164	204	141	117	175	213
	5h30	9h00	1h55	11h55	7h20	6h40	6h05	13h25	•	4h05	2h30	7h50	6h35	8h10	5h40	4h40	7h00	8h30
Pafuri Gate	380	109	287	76	438	246	392	•	335	250	312	434	172	444	380	218	415	453
	15h10	4h20	11h30	3h00	17h30	9h50	15h40	•	13h25	10h00	12h30	17h20	6h55	17h45	15h10	8h45	16h35	18h10
Paul Kruger Gate	12	283	104	354	60	224	•	392	152	158	119	65	220	74	53	173	88	83
	0h30	11h20	4h10	14h10	2h25	9h00	•	15h40	6h05	6h20	4h45	2h35	8h50	3h00	2h10	6h55	3h30	3h20
Phalaborwa Gate	213	137	119	201	261	•	224	246	167	83	145	267	74	277	213	51	246	285
	8h30	5h30	4h45	8h00	10h25	•	9h00	9h50	6h40	3h20	5h50	10h40	3h00	11h05	8h30	2h00	9h50	11h25
Pretoriuskop	49	318	140	389	•	261	60	438	184	195	156	9	258	85	90	211	125	92
	2h00	12h45	5h35	15h35	•	10h25	2h25	17h30	7h20	7h50	6h15	0h20	10h20	3h25	3h35	8h25	5h00	3h40
Punda Maria	342	71	245	•	389	201	354	76	297	212	274	396	130	408	342	176	377	415
	13h40	2h50	9h50	•	15h35	8h00	14h10	3h00	11h55	8h30	11h00	15h50	5h10	16h20	13h40	7h00	15h05	16h35
Satara	93	178	•	245	140	119	104	287	48	54	25	147	116	156	93	69	127	165
	3h45	7h10	•	9h50	5h35	4h45	4h10	11h30	1h55	2h10	1h00	5h55	4h40	6h15	3h45	2h45	5h05	6h35
Shingwedzi	271	•	178	71	318	137	283	109	226	141	203	325	63	333	271	109	306	344
	10h50	•	7h10	2h50	12h45	5h30	11h20	4h20	9h00	5h40	8h10	13h00	2h30	13h20	10h50	4h20	12h15	13h45
Skukuza	•	271	93	342	49	213	12	380	137	147	108	54	209	64	43	162	77	72
	•	10h50	3h45	13h40	2h00	8h30	0h30	15h10	5h30	5h55	4h20	2h10	8h20	2h35	1h45	6h30	3h05	2h55

HOW TO GET TO THE KRUGER NATIONAL PARK

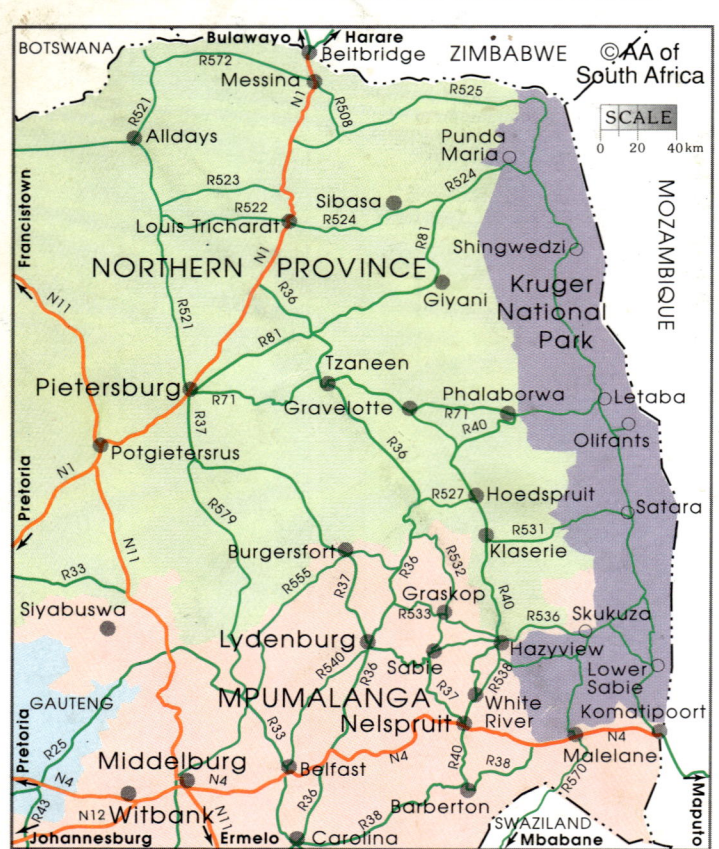

© AA of South Africa

DISTANCES AND APPROXIMATE TIMES TAKEN BETWEEN PRIVATE/BUSHVELD REST CAMPS AND NEARBY MAIN REST CAMPS

Time estimated travelling at 25 km/h

		DISTANCE	TIME
Bateleur	Mopani	65	2h35
	Shingwedzi	30	1h30
Biyamiti	Malelane	39	1h30
Boulders	Mopani	33	1h20
	Phalaborwa	54	2h10
Jakkalsbessie	Skukuza	5	0h10
Jock of the Bushveld	Malelane	33	1h20
	Skukuza	36	1h25
Roodewal	Olifants	30	1h10
	Satara	45	1h50
Shimuwini	Mopani	45	1h50
	Letaba	66	2h40
Sirheni	Punda Maria	54	2h10
	Shingwedzi	35	1h25
Talamati	Orpen	30	1h10
	Satara	52	2h05

KEY

Main rest camp	
Other rest camp	
Trail base camp	
Entrance gate	
Look-out point	
Get-out point	
Main picnic place	
Historical sites	32
Geological sites	32
Water point	
Mountain	
Altitude of mountain	366
Main road	H1-8
Secondary road	H5
Sand road	S8
Private road (no entry)	
Distance marker	
River	
Dam	
Local boundary	
International boundary	

Scale 0 — 2,5 — 5 km

Created by Jacana Education and the Kruger National Park

The publishers welcome any comments. Every reasonable care has been taken to ensure that the information on this Map was correct at the time of completion. Nevertheless, neither the Kruger National Park nor the publishers can accept responsibility for errors or omissions, or for changes in the details given. All rights reserved. No part of this publication may be reproduced, by any means whatsoever, without prior written permission of the publishers.

DTP Origination: Jacana Education, Johannesburg
Illustrations: Glynis Clouston, Joan Beuche, Sally MacLarty
Cover Photograph: Anthony Bannister Photo Library
Lithographic Repro: Remata Bureau, Johannesburg
Printing: Fishwick Printers, Durban

Published by
Jacana Education, Johannesburg 1998
P.O. Box 2004, Houghton 2041, South Africa
Tel: (011) 648-1157/487-1044 Fax: (011) 648-5516
© Jacana Education

ISBN 1-874955-90-5

9 781874 955900